W9-ASU-905

This book belongs to

_____

*In all these things we are more than conquerors through Christ who loves us.* Romans 8:37

Listen to and sing along with the Dramatic Reading and Songs for the Journey CDs.

Order from Great Commission Publications at
www.childrenspilgrimsprogress.org or 800-695-3387.

# PILGRIM'S PROGRESS

*John Bunyan's Classic Story Adapted for Children*

WRITTEN BY
## Anna Trimiew

ILLUSTRATED BY
## Drew Rose

GREAT COMMISSION
PUBLICATIONS

Writer, Anna Trimiew
(based on John Bunyan's classic story)

Theological Editor and *Pilgrim's Progress* Consultant,
John L. Musselman, The Jackson Institute

Illustrator, Drew Rose


Executive Director, Marvin Padgett

Director of Publications, Mark L. Lowrey, Jr.

Production Manager and Editor, Donnajo C. Williams

Assistant Production Manager, Heather Cossar

Art Director, Cynthia McBrayer

Copyright © 2014 by Great Commission Publications

Curriculum Edition First Printing: 2014

Printed in the United States of America

Great Commission Publications is the joint publishing ministry of the Committee
on Christian Education of the Orthodox Presbyterian Church and the Committee for
Christian Education & Publications of the Presbyterian Church in America.


All rights reserved. No part of this publication may be reproduced, stored
in a retrieval system or transmitted in any form by any means, digital,
mechanical, photocopy, recording or otherwise, without prior permission of
the publisher, except as provided for by USA copyright law.

**GREAT COMMISSION**
**PUBLICATIONS**

3640 Windsor Park Drive
Suwanee, GA 30024-3897
www.childrenspilgrimsprogress.org
800-695-3387

# TABLE OF CONTENTS

# ABOUT THIS BOOK

John Bunyan wrote his beloved classic *The Pilgrim's Progress* in two parts, the first published in London in 1678 and the second part in 1684. He originally titled it *The Pilgrim's Progress from This World to That Which Is to Come*. This book is a young reader's adaptation of the first part of Bunyan's book.

This version is designed to capture children's imaginations and introduce them to Bunyan's enduring masterpiece. The story will captivate them as they follow Christian on his adventurous journey as well as teach them great biblical truths they can hold onto as they grow in faith.

Some of the scenes have been condensed, and the language has been rewritten to appeal to children. But the essence of the story is the same: one Christian's walk of faith to the glorious goal.

Children will discover many important truths, including:
- a deeper understanding of Christ and the gospel
- the necessity of God's Word, the Holy Spirit, and other believers for teaching, instruction, encouragement, and support
- the true definition of a Christian
- a picture of the Christian life—a pilgrim's journey with ups and downs, distractions, difficulties, and even feelings of being cut off from God as a believer presses toward the grand end
- insight into the heart and character of Christians versus those who only claim to know Christ or reject him

Your child may not remember all the details nor grasp all the allegorical concepts, but we pray they will come to love the story and truths that it illustrates. Sowing this seed early will cause them to read the story again and again as they grow in faith and find encouragement and help in their own ongoing pilgrim's progress.

# INTRODUCTION

 long, long time ago, a prisoner sat in a cold jail in England. In his cell, he had a Bible, a pen, and some paper. Over many months, he wrote an adventure story that, in many ways, was like his own life. The man's name was John Bunyan, and his story became a famous book called *The Pilgrim's Progress*.

John was born in 1628 to a poor family in Bedford, England. When he was old enough, he learned to read and write at the village school. But soon he had to leave school to help his family. He became a tinker like his dad. A tinker is a person who mends pots and pans.

*Birthplace of John Bunyan*

Even though his family didn't have very much, John's early years were happy. From time to time though, he had very bad dreams and nightmares.

When John was older, he joined the army and fought in a war for England. After the war, John got married to a woman named Margaret. They had four children.

But John was troubled. He had a hard time believing in God. His wife told him about God's love and forgiveness. John came to trust in the Savior and have peace in his heart. After he put his faith in Christ, he joined a church in his hometown of Bedford. However, it wasn't the official state church, called the Church of England. During this time, John discovered that he had a gift for preaching God's Word.

John's wife died at a young age, and a few years later, he married his second wife, Elizabeth. By this time, he had become a popular preacher. But since John didn't belong to the Church of England, he was arrested and put in jail for preaching.

Elizabeth was a brave Christian. She tried all she could to get John out of prison. But he had to remain there for 12 years. After he was let go, he went back to the church in Bedford and continued preaching. He also helped start many other churches. But in a few years, he was again arrested and sent to jail. This time, he was freed in just a few months.

In 1688, John traveled to London. On the way home he got very sick. He stayed at a friend's house hoping to get better, but died there several days later. His family and friends took him to Bunhill Fields in London to bury him.

John will always be best remembered for his story *The Pilgrim's Progress*. In the hundreds of years since John wrote it, many people all over the world have read and treasured it. It has been translated into over 200 languages. The Bible is the only book that has ever sold more copies.

*The Pilgrim's Progress* is an allegory. An allegory is a story with two meanings. First, this is an exciting adventure story of a man and his friends on a journey to a wonderful place. On their way, they meet many challenges, dangers, and enemies. But it's also a story that teaches important truths about Jesus and every Christian's journey through life.

Now turn the pages! *The Pilgrim's Progress* has been rewritten especially for you to understand and enjoy.

# Chapter One

## *The Adventure Begins*

O h, what must I do?" cried a man dressed in rags as he walked in the fields outside his house. "What must I do?" he sadly cried again.

The man was carrying a heavy burden on his back and reading a book. "This book says the city I live in, the City of Destruction, will be burned one day with fire from heaven. I must find a way to escape! Oh, what must I do? Where should I go?" The man anxiously looked this way and that, not knowing what to do.

Just then, a man named Evangelist came up to him. "Why are you crying?" he asked kindly.

"Sir," replied the troubled, ragged man, "this book tells me that I am condemned to die and after that there will be judgment. I'm afraid that this huge, heavy burden on my back will cause me to fall into hell. Thinking about such things makes me cry!"

"If you feel this way, then why are you still standing here?" Evangelist asked.

"Because I don't know where to go."

Evangelist was someone who taught people about the gospel. He handed the man a scroll, which was something like a map. The scroll said, "Run away from the destruction to come."

"Do you see that small Wicket Gate over there?" Evangelist asked as he pointed beyond the fields.

"No."

"Do you see that Shining Light?"

"I think I do," the man said.

"Keep your eye on that Light," Evangelist smiled. "It will lead you to the gate. When you get there, knock, and someone will tell you what to do. So dry your tears and go quickly!"

The man began to run away from the City of Destruction toward the Light. His wife and children cried out for him to return. But he put his fingers in his ears and cried out, "Life! Life! Life that lasts forever!" And Christian, for that was his name, did not look back.

Some people from the city saw him running off. Many made fun of him and thought he was going crazy.

Two neighbors decided to go after Christian and bring him back. The name of one was Obstinate and the name of the other was Pliable. Their names said a lot about them. Obstinate was a very stubborn man, and Pliable would go along with anyone who had a new idea.

"Come back with us," they begged.

"No," Christian said, shaking his head. "You should come with me, away from the City of Destruction. I'm going to a wonderful place, where we may live forever. You can read about it in this book. Everything in this book is true."

But Obstinate refused. "No, I'm going home," he said. And he tried to get Pliable to go back with him.

But Pliable said, "If what Christian says is true, I will go with him."

"Very well, then," Obstinate said crossly. "I'll gladly leave you two dreamers!" And with a toss of his head, the stubborn fellow turned back toward the City of Destruction.

# CHAPTER TWO

## *Christian Gets Into Trouble*

hristian and Pliable walked across the fields, talking as they went. "Tell me more about the place where we're going," Pliable said.

"Since you are curious, I will read to you from my book," Christian said happily. "It tells about a wonderful kingdom that will never end. We'll receive beautiful crowns. We will get clothes that will make us shine like the sun. There will be no more crying and sadness and . . ."

"That sounds wonderful," Pliable interrupted. "Come on! Let's walk faster!"

"I wish I could, but I can't go any faster with this heavy burden on my back," Christian replied.

As they talked, they came near a muddy place called

the Slough of Despond, a mucky swamp. But they weren't paying attention and both slipped, falling into the grimy, thick water.

"Where are you?" cried Pliable.

"I don't know!" shouted Christian. He tried to climb out but sank deeper and deeper because of his burden. It was a dangerous place, and they were scared.

Then Pliable became very angry. "It's all your fault we're in this mess," he complained. "If it's this awful at the beginning, what else is it going to be like? I'm going back home. You can look for that new, wonderful place all by yourself!"

Pliable struggled but finally climbed out of the swamp. Dirty and wet, he left and turned toward home. But Christian, scared and alone, was still stuck in the swamp and thought he might drown.

Just then, a man named Help came along. "Look! Don't you see these steppingstones?" he asked Christian. "Give me your hand."

Help lifted the tired pilgrim out of the mud. "This swamp cannot be fixed," he explained. "It is full of all the fears and doubts of a person when he begins to realize he is a sinner. When all the dirt and mud from sin is stirred up, you can barely see the steps."

Safe from the swamp, Christian continued alone on his journey. He came across a man named Mr. Worldly Wiseman, who lived in a town near the City of Destruction. Worldly had heard all about the pilgrim and his journey. "Hello there, my good fellow!" he said.

"Where are you going with that heavy burden?"

"I'm going to that gate," Christian answered, pointing ahead. "A man named Evangelist told me to go this way to get my burden removed."

"Bad advice!" Worldly said with a laugh. "There's not a more dangerous path in the world than this one. That swamp you just went through is only the beginning of the troubles that lie ahead! You'll face many dangers, darkness, and . . . and . . . death!

"I don't care what I meet along the way if I also can get rid of this burden," Christian said firmly.

Worldly asked him, "How did you get this burden?" Christian replied, "By reading this book in my hand."

Worldly snickered and said, "I thought so. You need to follow my advice and take a shorter path. Go and see a man named Legality. He will remove your burden. If he's not at home, his son, Civility, will help you. Legality lives close by in the next village called Morality. Go by that mountain over there, and the first house you come to is his."

Christian walked with heavy steps toward the man's house. What he didn't know was that Legality insisted that by keeping the Ten Commandments and being good you could be rescued from destruction. Worldly didn't tell Christian that no person has ever been able to keep the Ten Commandments or be good enough.

So, as Christian continued on, flashes of fire appeared on the mountain, called Mt. Sinai. Christian was afraid he would be burned. His burden seemed to grow heavier. He was sorry that he had followed Mr. Worldly Wiseman's advice. He was so scared that he stood still, not knowing whether to go forward or backward. He broke out in a sweat.

At that moment, Evangelist walked up. "What are you doing here?" he asked Christian in surprise. "Aren't you the man I found crying outside the City of Destruction?"

"Yes, sir. I am," said Christian, filled with shame.

"Didn't I tell you to stay on the path to the gate?" Evangelist asked.

"Yes, but I met a man who told me that path was wrong. He told me how to get rid of my burden quickly," Christian said, his voice cracking. "He also said he would show me a better path than the one you set me on."

"I know Worldly Wiseman. He is a wicked man," Evangelist said, shaking his head. "He turned you from the right way. He showed you a path that would have destroyed you. There are three things you must hate about Worldly Wiseman's advice:

1. how he tries to get you off the right path,
2. how he tries to make you hate the Cross, and
3. how he points you to the wrong road—one that leads to death!

"As for Mr. Legality, he couldn't free you from your burden of sin by keeping the law. He's trying to trick you."

As Christian stood trembling under his burden, Evangelist showed him words in the book, God's words. "Jesus your Lord and King says that the road is narrow and the gate is small that leads to life, and that only a few find it."

"Oh, can my sin be forgiven?" Christian cried. "Is there any hope that I may now go back and find the right path and the gate?"

"Yes! Your sin is great, for you got off the narrow path. But the man at the gate will receive you, for he is kind and merciful."

Then Evangelist hugged Christian and sent him on his way. "Don't get off the narrow way again," he warned, as the pilgrim hurriedly turned around to go back to the right path. Christian didn't speak to anyone else until he got back to the right road leading to the gate.

# CHAPTER THREE

## *Interpreter's House and the Place of Deliverance*

hristian stayed on the right path, and soon he came to the gate, just as Evangelist had said. Christian stopped when he saw the words above the door of the gate. "Knock, and the door will be opened to you," he read. So he began knocking loudly.

At last, a man named Goodwill appeared. "Who's there?" he asked. "What do you want?"

Christian replied, "I'm a poor burdened sinner. I've come from the City of Destruction, but I'm going to a wonderful place called the Celestial City to live with the King. Are you willing to let me in?"

"Oh, yes, with all my heart!" And with that, Goodwill opened the gate and quickly pulled Christian inside. Goodwill knew that the Evil Prince named Beelzebub would shoot arrows at those outside the gate, hoping they would die before they could get in.

"I'm so glad I'm out of danger and that you allowed me in," sighed Christian.

"Tell me," Goodwill continued. "I want to hear all about your journey so far. What have you learned?" Christian told him about the things that had happened and the people he'd met. Then Goodwill instructed, "Now look ahead. Do you see that narrow road, straight as a ruler? That is the way you must go."

"But . . . but are there any twists and turns?" Christian wanted to know. "Will I lose my way?"

"There are many crooked and wide paths that go off the right path," Goodwill explained. "But you can tell the right way from the wrong ones because the right path is always straight and narrow. Now, continue on and you will come to a house. A man named Interpreter will show you many excellent things!

"Oh, and about your burden," Goodwill added. "You'll have to carry it until you come to the Place of Deliverance. Then it will fall off by itself!"

Christian then prepared himself for the journey ahead. He said goodbye to Goodwill and walked on. The morning was bright and beautiful. Birds sang cheerfully. The air was fresh and sweet.

Soon he came to a large house. Christian knocked and called out, "I'm on my way to the Celestial City. I'm looking for Interpreter, a man who will warn me of dangers and explain important things that will help me on my journey."

"Come in," said Interpreter as he opened the door. "I will show you seven rooms in this house and tell you what they mean." First, Interpreter pointed to a picture. It was of a serious man with a crown on his head. His eyes were lifted up to heaven, and in his hands he held the best book in the world. "The Lord has sent this one," Interpreter explained. "He is a pastor—a true and faithful servant of the Master. Your pastor will teach you how to face hard situations on your journey."

Pastor

Then Interpreter led him to a second room that was filled with dust. At Interpreter's command, the room was swept, but the dust just swirled around and didn't go away. Then Interpreter commanded the dusty room to be sprinkled with water. Now it was shining and clean!

"What does this mean?" asked Christian. The Interpreter explained that the heart of a person is clogged with the dust of sin. Only the gospel of grace can get rid of it. God gives a person a new and clean heart by his grace. His new heart makes him ready to put his trust in the King of glory.

After that, they went into the third room, where two children named Passion and Patience sat in chairs. "Passion is impatient. He wants everything now," the Interpreter said, shaking his head sadly. "He is greedy. He wasted a big bag of treasure. Now he has nothing left but rags.

"On the other hand," he added brightly, "Patience is willing to wait for the best things, especially those that will come later." Interpreter told Christian not to covet things that are in the present but to wait patiently for what Christ will give you, and be thankful.

The fourth room was a little scary at first. There was a fire burning against a wall. A man with a bottle of water kept trying to put out the fire, but it wouldn't go out.

Interpreter took Christian to the other side of the wall, where a man continuously threw oil on the fire to keep it burning. He explained, "The first man is the devil. He tries to destroy the faith of a pilgrim but can't ever do it. The second man is Christ. He secretly and continuously throws the oil of grace on the heart of a pilgrim to strengthen his faith."

Then, Interpreter showed him the fifth room. In it was a tall, guarded door to a beautiful palace beyond. This was a glimpse of heaven, the place God has prepared by his grace for pilgrims who trust in Jesus. "Remember," warned Interpreter, "keep going on your journey even when it gets dangerous and hard."

Then they entered a dark room, where a Caged Man sat. "Who are you?" Christian asked.

"I'm a miserable man and I've lost hope. I've sinned against God, against his Spirit, and against his Word. I've hardened my heart against God and I cannot repent."

"What did you do to bring yourself to this condition?" inquired Christian.

"I didn't keep watch," the man sighed. "I followed the empty pleasures of this world. Now they nibble at me like worms that burn when they bite!" Interpreter said that the Caged Man was a warning to Christian not to harden his heart against God and his Word.

Christian turned away, saying quietly, "God, help me to keep watch over my heart and not follow the ways of the world."

Then they came to the last room. Here they saw a shaking, trembling man, who told them about a dream he had. Interpreter explained, "His dream was about Christ coming again. It was a warning about the last judgment. The dreamer was afraid because he wasn't sure he was ready for the Day of Judgment."

Now it was time for Christian to continue on his journey. Interpreter asked, "Have you thought about these lessons?"

"Yes, and I am hopeful but also somewhat afraid."

"Keep all the things you have learned in your mind to remind you when you are tempted to get off the narrow way. And remember that the Comforter—the Holy Spirit—will be with you always to guide you in the way that leads to the Celestial City."

The pilgrim then went on his way. The road was fenced with a wall called Salvation. He started running, although it was difficult with the heavy load on his back. Breathing hard, he came to a hill and looked up. On that hill stood a Cross, and just as he came to it, his burden came loose and fell off his back. It rolled all the

way to the bottom of the hill into a grave, where it disappeared forever!

The King of the Celestial City had removed the weight of sin from his shoulders at the Place of Deliverance. "Jesus has given me rest from my sadness and life through his death," Christian cried, his eyes glued to the Cross. Tears of joy and wonder streamed down his cheeks. He stood still for a long while to gaze in awe.

Just then, three Shining Ones came to him. The first one said, "Your sins are forgiven." The second one removed the rags he was wearing and put beautiful clothes on him. Then the third Shining One set a mark on his forehead and gave him a rolled-up paper document with a seal on it.

"Take care of this document and read it for comfort as you go on your way," the third Shining One told Christian. "You'll be asked to turn it in at the gate of the Celestial City." After this, the Shining Ones left.

Christian gave three leaps for joy. Then he started singing a wonderful song about all that the Man on the Cross had suffered for him. He sang how his burden had rolled off as soon as he came up to the Cross. Feeling light as air, Christian continued singing happily as he went on his way.

# Chapter Four

## *The Hill of Difficulty and House Beautiful*

s Christian, now free of his burden, continued to walk, he saw three men asleep by the side of the road. They had turned away from the narrow path. He woke them up and told them they were in danger. "The Evil Prince goes around like a roaring lion. He waits for people like you!" Christian warned. But they were lazy, thought they were just fine, and paid no attention. They soon fell asleep again.

Farther on, two men jumped over the wall on one side of the narrow way. "Where did you come from and where are you going?" Christian asked.

The men said they were from the land of Boasting, a place where people bragged about how good they were. "We're on our way to the Celestial City," they declared.

"But . . . but you should have come in at the gate!" Christian said.

"Oh," they said boldly. "We wanted to take a shortcut, so we went across the fields and came over the wall. Don't worry, we'll be just fine!"

"Don't you know that the book says that if you don't come in by the gate, and if you come in another way, you are a thief and a robber? Since you came to this path by yourselves and didn't follow the King's directions," Christian said gently but firmly, "you'll have to leave it by yourselves without the King's mercy."

Then the pilgrim explained how the Lord had taken away his rags and heavy burden, and given him the beautiful clothes, the mark on his forehead, and the rolled document with a seal. But the two laughed at Christian. They told him to mind his own business.

Christian walked on ahead of them. Sometimes he felt God's comfort. At other times he felt discouraged. He often read from the document that the Shining Ones had given him, and that made him feel better.

Soon the three came to the Hill of Difficulty. Christian began to climb up the straight and narrow way. Two other paths went around the bottom of the hill that looked a lot easier than the high hill. One of the men foolishly took the path called Destruction. The other took the path called Danger.

The hill was very steep, and Christian had to climb on his hands and knees. He then came to a shady place provided by the King for travelers to rest. He sat down and read his document for comfort. He fell fast asleep, and the document fell out of his hand.

It began to get dark. Just then, someone woke him up and warned him to get on his way. Christian quickly jumped to his feet and ran up the hill. Before he reached the top, two men named Mistrust and Fearful hurried toward him.

"You're going the wrong way!" Christian said.

"The further we go, the more danger we find. So we're going back home," Fearful said, his voice trembling.

"Yes," added Mistrust, "up ahead there are a couple of ferocious lions. They might tear us to pieces!"

"If I go forward, I may face death," said Christian firmly. "But beyond the fear of death is life that lasts forever, so I'll keep going forward."

Christian reached for his document, but it wasn't there. He fell to his knees. He asked God to forgive him for losing the document, which was his pass into the Celestial City. He went back to look for it, tears streaming down his face. "Oh, what a foolish man I am!" he cried. "I lost the document that comforted me so much. Now it will be night before I make it to the top of the hill."

Back in the resting place, Christian found what he was looking for. He put the precious document safely inside his coat, over his heart. He thanked God for showing him where to find it. Then he turned and hurried up the hill.

He saw two scary lions, and beyond that a beautiful house. The Watchman of the house, a doorkeeper, called out to him to not be afraid of the lions because they were chained. He told Christian that the lions were there to test whether a pilgrim really had faith or not. Trembling with fear, Christian did what the man said and safely passed by the two chained lions. He heard them roar, but they could not harm him.

"Sir, what place is this?" Christian asked the doorkeeper.

"This is House Beautiful. It was built by the King to give pilgrims relief and protection while on their way to the Celestial City," said the man, leading him to the front door.

"My name is Christian," he introduced

himself, "but it used to be Graceless."

Soon, a wise lady named Discretion came out and questioned the pilgrim. She asked how he became a Christian and what he had experienced on his journey. Then she was joined by Prudence, Piety, and Charity. They too asked him about his journey.

"Come in, come in," they said at last, pleased with his answers. "With the King's blessing, come in!" Once inside, they continued talking until supper was ready.

"What else did you learn along the way?" they asked Christian.

"I learned that Satan cannot stop Jesus Christ our King from doing his good work of grace in our hearts," he said. The women asked him whether he was still tempted to do sinful things, and he admitted that he was. He said that several things helped him have victory over his desire to sin: remembering what Jesus had done on the Cross, seeing his new life in Jesus, and reading the book that Jesus had given him. And, finally, he said that it helped him not to give into temptation when he remembered that he was going to the Celestial City.

Some people were listening to the conversation. They agreed entirely. "Christ the King loves poor pilgrims very much," they said. "There isn't anyone like him to be found from the east to the west!"

After a hearty supper, the conversation continued until late. They talked about what Jesus had done and why. They said he was the great Warrior who fought and conquered Satan by pouring out his own blood.

They prayed and then went to bed. Christian slept very well in a pleasant bedroom called Peace.

The next day the Watchman and the women took Christian to the study. They read many true and amazing stories about the Lord and what he had done for and through his servants like Moses and David.

Then they took him to the armory. They showed him protective equipment the Lord provides pilgrims: swords, shields, helmets, breastplates, and just the right shoes for the journey. Christian also saw the rod of Moses, the jawbone Samson used to do mighty deeds, the sling and stone David used to kill the enemy Goliath, and many other things. They also showed him a faraway view of a beautiful place called the Delectable Mountains that he would come to in his journey down the road.

"Now you must put on God's armor to protect you from any attacks along the way," Discretion and the others said. And there they fitted him from head to foot with just the right things to protect him.

With this done, it was time for Christian to travel on. They stepped out on a rocky path. "It's just as hard to go down the hill as it was to climb up it, for you are going down into the Valley of Humiliation," Prudence said, when she saw Christian stumble a time or two. His friends gave him bread, raisins, and something to drink. And Christian went on his way.

# CHAPTER FIVE

## *Through Dark Valleys*

hristian had only walked a short distance when he entered the Valley of Humiliation. He saw a huge, evil monster named Apollyon coming toward him. He was covered with scales like a fish. He had wings like a dragon, feet like a bear, and a mouth like a lion. Out of his stomach poured fire and smoke.

Christian was scared to death and felt like running away. But he quickly decided to stand his ground. "Where have you come from?" growled Apollyon.

"I've come from the City of Destruction, which is a place of evil," Christian answered.

"I'm the prince of that city, so you are a subject of mine! Why have you run away from me?" Apollyon roared. "I should strike you down to the ground with one blow!"

"I was born in your kingdom," Christian said. "But I now serve someone else, the King over all. I've given him my faith and loyalty. How can I go back on my word?"

"You've already been unfaithful to him," accused Apollyon. "You fell in the Slough of Despond. You tried to get rid of your burden the wrong way. You slept and lost that document of yours. The lions almost scared you off, and you're always boasting about your journey!"

"You're right about all that, and even more," Christian nodded. "Yet my King is kind and has forgiven me."

"Serve me instead. My pay is better!"

"I know what you pay, Apollyon," Christian declared. "You pay the wages of sin, which is death."

Then the evil monster became very angry. "I'm the enemy of this King," he said in a rage. "I hate him, his laws, and his people. Prepare to die!"

"Be careful, Apollyon," warned Christian as he held up his shield. "I'm on the King's highway, the holy way!"

Then with a terrible howl, Apollyon attacked Christian. He shot a flaming arrow at him, but Christian held up his shield of faith and blocked the arrow. The monster kept shooting arrows at Christian, wounding him in many places. The battle lasted half a day and Christian grew weaker and weaker as he fought valiantly with his sword. Finally, Apollyon rushed toward the pilgrim and wrestled him to the ground. Christian's sword fell out of his hand.

"I'll win the battle!" the evil creature yelled as he almost crushed Christian to death.

"Not so fast, my enemy!" Christian gasped as he made a last desperate effort and grabbed his sword. "Though I've fallen, I shall rise!" With that, he gave Apollyon a deadly thrust upward into the monster's stomach. Apollyon howled in pain and stumbled backwards. Christian quickly attacked him a second time, crying out, "No, in all these things we are more than conquerors—through Christ who loved us." At that, the evil one spread his dragon's wings and flew away across the Valley of Humiliation. Christian didn't see him anymore in the valley.

Christian wearily sat down to rest. A hand came to him with leaves from the Tree of Life. Christian used the leaves to cover the bleeding cuts and wounds on his body, and they were healed right away.

"The King strengthened me against Apollyon and healed my wounds," Christian said thankfully. Then he took a drink and ate some bread. When he felt a little stronger, he got up. With his sword drawn, he left one valley to enter another, scarier than the one he just left, and more lonely.

As he arrived at the Valley of the Shadow of Death, two men ran toward him. "Go back quickly," they cried. "If you value your life or peace, come with us!"

"Why?" asked Christian. "What's the matter?"

"The valley is as dark as night. It's the most awful place," they trembled. "It's full of terrible creatures, which all howl and yell in misery. It's *really* scary!"

"The narrow way to the King and the Celestial City leads straight through it," Christian said, leaving the frightened men. "So I must go on."

The pathway was dark and very narrow. On one side there was a deep ditch and on the other side, a dangerous swamp. Christian was afraid and took one small step after another very slowly. Screams filled the air. Flames and puffs of smoke shot up all around him through the creepy fog. It was more frightening than anything he had experienced so far. He realized that he couldn't fight this danger with his sword, so he pulled out another weapon of his armor, called All-Prayer. He prayed, "O Lord, please deliver my soul!"

A pack of wild beasts appeared and looked like they might tear him to pieces, so he yelled, "I will walk in the strength of the Lord!" At that, they backed off into the darkness.

Christian kept walking, almost falling into the mouth of a burning pit. There, he heard a voice behind his ear whispering naughty, bad words. Was it one of the Wicked Ones whispering the horrible thoughts or did the words come from his own mind? Oh, how troubled Christian was to think that he could have such terrible thoughts against the Lord he loved! Christian was more confused and discouraged than he had ever been in his life. But he kept on walking as carefully as he could along the narrow path.

After some time had passed, Christian thought he heard a voice up ahead, saying, "Even though I walk through the valley of the shadow of death, I will fear no evil, for you, Lord, are with me." Christian was glad that another pilgrim who loved Jesus was in this valley. He called out to him, but there was no answer. Christian hoped that he could soon catch up with him.

Time passed and morning came. Christian looked back to see what dangers he had gone through in the darkness. Now he saw more clearly how narrow the path was that led between the ditch and the bog. He saw the fearful creatures of the burning pit. Then Christian looked ahead at the path before him. It was full of even more dangers, traps, pits, and deep holes. But Christian began singing, "Christ's lamp shines on my head, and by his light I go through darkness" as he walked on. Christian finally came to the end of the dark valleys.

# CHAPTER SIX

## *Christian Meets Faithful*

hristian saw another pilgrim named Faithful on the road ahead of him. "Wait for me and I'll walk with you," Christian shouted.

But Faithful would not stop. "Enemies are behind me and I'm running for my life!" he called back.

Christian began to run as fast as he could. He caught up with Faithful and ran past him, showing off a little. But he didn't look where he was going and suddenly stumbled and fell. Faithful helped him up.

"My friend," began Faithful, "I meant to travel with you when you left the City of Destruction. But you left so suddenly! After you were gone, there was much talk about you, and how our city would burn with fire from heaven. Our neighbors didn't believe the news. But I believed it, and so I escaped!"

"Was there any talk of our neighbor Pliable?"

"He is much worse off than if he had never left the City. People laugh at him and call him a coward because he turned back at the first bit of trouble he ran into."

"I'm afraid he'll die when the City of Destruction is burned up," Christian said sadly. "But now let's talk about what's happened to you on the narrow way."

Faithful replied, "I didn't fall into that awful swamp—the Slough of Despond. I did meet a woman who tried to make me turn aside with her to do impure things. But I refused. Then I met an old man who asked me to live with him. But I realized that he wanted to make me a slave."

"And then what?" asked Christian.

"I tried to leave, but the man jerked me back, hurting me. When I got halfway up the hill, another man ran up and knocked me down. Every time I got up he knocked me down again even when I cried for mercy. But he had no mercy. He would have killed me, but someone else came by and made him stop."

"Who made him stop?"

"I wasn't sure at first," Faithful said quietly. "But when I saw the holes in his hands and side, then I knew it was the Lord Jesus. He delivered me!"

"Did you see the House Beautiful?"

"Yes, and the chained lions too. But they were asleep," said Faithful. "I didn't stop there but kept going. I met two men named Discontent and Shame in the Valley of Humiliation. Discontent was unhappy with everyone and everything and tried to persuade me to go back. He said I would offend all my old friends, like Mr. Pride and Mr. Conceited, if I kept going. And Mr. Shame made fun of religion. He said it was shameful to feel badly if I did something wrong and asked for forgiveness."

"Yes," Christian said, "I've heard Shame wants to make us ashamed of what is good, but we have to keep resisting him, telling him he is wrong."

Faithful replied, "I think we will have to cry out to Jesus for help against him. What God says is best even if all the men in the world are against it."

"Yes, you are right!" continued Christian. "I had a horrible fight with that awful creature Apollyon in the Valley of Humiliation. But I cried out to God and he gave me the strength to fight him off. Then I entered the dreadful Valley of the Shadow of Death. I thought I would die there, but finally the morning came. And I walked through the rest of the valley with ease!"

The path became wider than usual. Suddenly a man appeared. "Say there," Faithful called out, "are you on your way to the Celestial City?"

"Yes," answered Talkative, for that was his name. He was tall and handsome.

Talkative happily began to walk along with them.

Then he chatted on and on for a long time about God and heaven. After a while, Faithful went over to Christian and said to him softly, "What a fine man this is. He will make a very good pilgrim."

"Don't you know him? Talkative lives in our city. He pretends to be a pilgrim, but he's not. He just likes to talk like he is," Christian explained. "Away from home, he talks big, but at home he doesn't pray, and he complains all the time; he even gets violent. He acts like a Christian in public, but he treats his family in awful ways."

Christian told Faithful to ask Talkative some questions that would show what he was really like. So Faithful said, "Since you talk so much about the saving grace of God, how does it show itself in a person's heart and the way he lives?"

"Well, it should make a person be bold to talk against sin . . . ," Talkative began.

"Don't you think it should really cause someone to hate his own sin not just talk about it?" Faithful asked.

Talkative was upset about Faithful's question. "What difference does it make? It really shouldn't matter to you! I think you are trying to trap me!" he said.

"It does matter," replied Faithful. "Saying and doing are two different things. If you talk so much about God and his grace and goodness, you ought to be glad to do what he says!"

"Oh, I'll do as I like," Talkative said angrily. "You're not my judge!"

Faithful then explained, "Others can see how God's grace has changed a person in two ways:

1. that person personally confesses that he trusts in Christ alone to save him, and

2. that person lives a life that shows he belongs to Christ—desiring to do what God says.

"Your neighbors, Talkative, say that you cheat, lie, and harm many people by the ungodly way you live."

Talkative turned red and marched off angrily. Faithful and Christian then continued the journey alone.

Later, Evangelist caught up with them. Both men were very glad to see him. "My dear friends," he said, "what have you been through since I saw you last? How did you deal with what happened?"

The two pilgrims told him of all the things that had happened to them along the narrow way. Evangelist listened carefully. Then he smiled and said, "I'm so glad that you kept going on the narrow way through all the hard things you faced. You'll face more enemies and hardships yet, and one of you will face death. The one who dies will have it better than the one who does not because he will go straight to the Celestial City. The other will have to go through trials. Now guard your hearts carefully against temptation. Be faithful and depend on King Jesus! Remember that he is strong when you are weak. Remember where you are going—to the King in the Celestial City!"

# Chapter Seven

## *Vanity Fair*

Christian and Faithful kept walking and saw a town ahead. The way to the Celestial City went right through the town, which was named Vanity. And this town had a fair set up by the Wicked Prince and his evil helpers many years before.

All kinds of delightful things were sold at this fair, such as houses, honors, positions, pleasures, wives, husbands, children, silver, gold, and pearls. These were the same kinds of things Satan tempted Jesus with when he lived on earth. Satan offered to make Jesus the Lord of the Fair if he would only bow down to him, the Evil Prince. But Jesus resisted Satan's temptations with God's Word and left that fair.

The people in the fair wore the finest clothes and

were busy doing whatever they wanted to do, whether it was right or wrong. They only pleased themselves all day long. The fair was filled with all kinds of cheaters, fools, games, jugglers, and beggars.

When Faithful and Christian arrived, people made fun of the clothes they wore. Others laughed at how they talked. Still others were amazed that they did not want to buy any of the things for sale. People called them fools and troublemakers.

"You must buy something," one man said, frowning at the two pilgrims. "What do you plan to buy?"

"We only buy the truth. We are strangers and pilgrims in this world and are on our way to our true home, the Celestial City," they replied. "Now please let us continue on our journey."

The Vanity Fair people became very angry. They began to beat Faithful and Christian harshly. Then they put the pilgrims in a cage where everyone could see and say cruel things to them.

Faithful and Christian patiently sat there. They replied with wise and kind words when people were mean and ugly.

Even when the people put chains on them and marched them up and down the streets, the two pilgrims behaved even more wisely. When some people at the fair saw how good and kind they were, they began to take the side of Christian and Faithful.

This made the group against the pilgrims even more upset. They said the two should die for all the trouble they had caused. So the people brought them before Judge Hate-Good.

"These pilgrims are enemies of the town," they told the judge. "They are against our ruler, the Evil Prince, and have even won over a number of our people to their side!"

"I'm a peaceful man," Faithful said, looking at the judge. "But I will never serve your ruler, the Wicked Prince. He is the enemy of the King over all, the One whom I trust and obey."

Then Judge Hate-Good said, "Anyone who has something good to say about the Wicked Prince and something bad against Faithful, speak up!"

Envy, who was jealous of everyone, stepped forward. "Your Honor," he said to the judge, "this man Faithful is disobedient and argues all the time, and he does not honor our ruler!"

Superstition spoke next. "Your Honor, this man said we're all sinful and that what we believe and do doesn't please God."

Then Pick-thank spoke up. "I've known this fellow

for a long time," he said. "Faithful has not only spoken against our leader, the Wicked Prince, but he's said bad things about our leader's helpers, Mr. Old Man, Mr. Greedy, and the others.

"Besides that," Pick-thank went on, "he's not been afraid to speak against you, your Honor, saying that you don't trust and obey God."

"You rebel and traitor!" Judge Hate-Good yelled, turning to Faithful. "Have you heard what these men have said against you?"

"May I say a few words in my own defense?" Faithful asked quietly.

"You deserve to die right on the spot," said the judge angrily. "Yet, let's hear what you have to say first, so that everyone can see how well we've treated you."

"I said that anyone or anything in this town that is against God and his Word is fit for hell," Faithful said bravely. "Now, Lord, may you show me kindness!"

Then the judge sent the jury out. They soon decided that Faithful was guilty according to their law and sentenced him to death. The people cruelly beat him, stabbed him with knives and swords, and threw stones at him. Finally, they burned him at the stake.

As soon as Faithful died, a heavenly chariot came and carried him up through the clouds. He was taken straight to the gate of the Celestial City to the clear, bright sound of trumpets!

Meanwhile, the One who rules over everything helped Christian escape from the cage where he was kept. Christian quickly left the town of Vanity. Tears were in his eyes as he went on his way singing this song about his friend Faithful.

*Well, my friend, you spoke up for the King,*
*Now in heaven, his praises you'll sing!*
*Though they killed you, Faithful lives on,*
*From the Lord's side, you'll never be gone!*

# CHAPTER EIGHT

## *Hopeful Joins Christian*

hristian walked away from Vanity Fair, but he wasn't alone for long. A man named Hopeful left Vanity to catch up with Christian. He had seen and heard Christian and Faithful. He knew they spoke the truth and decided to go over to their side. He met up with Christian and promised to be his companion on the narrow way.

They walked along and soon came to a man named Mr. By-Ends. "Where are you from?" they asked.

"I'm from the town of Fairspeech," he said. "My friends and family are very rich people and have a very comfortable life." By-Ends was a proud man and loved his high position and easy life in a town where, sad to say, people tell lies all the time.

By-Ends continued, "In Fairspeech we are very religious, but not as strict as some people are. We don't believe in a religion that means you have to go through hard or dangerous things, and we like being religious when life is really easy, especially when other people approve of us."

Now Christian had read in the Bible about people who are not the King's true servants, so he said, "We can't travel together then. If you go with us and follow the King, you must go through hard times as well as easy. And, you must be willing to follow Christ whether you are poor or rich."

"Don't force me to believe the way you do," said By-Ends. "Let me walk with you and do what I want."

"Not a step further, unless you change your ways," Christian said firmly.

"Very well then," answered By-Ends. "Go on alone. I'll follow what I believe and wait until someone comes along who thinks like me."

Soon By-Ends was joined by three friends from his school days: Mr. Money-Love, Mr. Hold-onto-the-World, and Mr. Save-all. Their teacher, Mr. Gripeman, had taught them how to cheat, tell lies, and pretend to be religious. These friends used their reason to twist God's Word to defend the wrong things they believed.

"Who are those two men?" By-Ends' friends asked.

"Oh, they are pilgrims also," replied By-Ends, "but not our sort. If you disagree with them, they won't have anything to do with you. And they follow their King in all kinds of weather. They risk their lives for God, and stay on the path even when it's dangerous. I prefer to wait for good weather, and to make sure that I am always safe!"

By-Ends and his friends caught up to Christian and Hopeful and called out, "Let's talk some more. What's wrong with using religion and acting religious so we can get rich and have an easy life, if that is the only way we can do it?"

Christian said clearly, "Having money isn't a sin, but it's wrong to go after Christ because you hope that you'll get rich by following him. Only those who truly are against him would try to do that!"

The men were shocked at his answer and said nothing. They didn't walk with Christian and Hopeful anymore.

Christian and Hopeful kept going, across A Plain Called Ease, where they traveled in peace. Soon afterward, they came to a hill called Lucre. A man named Demas cried out, "Come over here and I will show you a rich silver mine. With a little hard work, you may get rich!"

"Let's go and see," said

Hopeful as he started to turn off the path.

But Christian pulled him back. "No!" he said. "I've heard of this place. The ground is shaky. Many have fallen into the mine and have been badly hurt or killed."

Then he called to Demas, "Isn't the place dangerous?"

"No . . . not really, if you're careful," said Demas, turning red because he was lying. "Please come over and see," he added with a quick smile.

But Christian said firmly, "Your silver mine is a trap for those who go after it. You've turned away from the narrow path and you're an enemy of the King! Besides, the King would hear the news if we left the narrow path for you, and we would be ashamed when we see him."

Demas kept calling out to them to come over, but the pilgrims went on their way. They said, "I bet By-Ends and his friends will go to Demas!"

Sure enough, a little while later, By-Ends and his friends came up and went right over to Demas. They were never ever seen again. Perhaps they fell into the pit or died in the bottom of that mine.

Soon, Christian and Hopeful came to a place where a strange, white statue of a woman stood by the roadside. Her face was turned away from the path. Written above her head were the words "Remember Lot's Wife!"

"I know what this is," Christian said. "God turned Lot's wife into a pillar of salt for disobeying his instructions not to look back when the wicked city of Sodom was destroyed."

"She is both a warning and an example to us," Hopeful realized. "I'm glad we didn't go off the path when Demas called us. We can thank God for warning us and we must never forget it."

Then the narrow path went right along the bank of a lovely river. There were trees with delicious fruit and a pretty green meadow filled with lilies and beautiful flowers. God had put this delightful place here for pilgrims who had been through many hard trials. Christian and Hopeful, tired from all their travels, rested in this peaceful spot.

While there, they drank cool water from the river. They ate fruit. They used the tree leaves God provided for medicine. They sang songs of joy and praise to the King. And each night they lay down in the meadow and slept safely.

After many days and nights of rest, food, and peace, the pilgrims felt strong and healthy once more. So, they went on their way, leaving the beautiful valley behind.

# Chapter Nine

## Giant Despair and Doubting Castle

he path away from the lovely river was rough and stony. The pilgrims were tired and their feet were very sore. On the left, a fence with steps over it divided the narrow way from a wide green meadow. There was a pretty, soft, grassy path in the meadow.

"Hopeful," said Christian, "let's walk over there. It looks a lot easier."

"But what if that path should lead us out of the narrow way?" asked Hopeful.

"Look, it runs close to the fence in the same direction," Christian answered. "We'll be fine!"

So, they climbed over the fence into By-Path Meadow onto the soft and easier path.

Christian called out to a man ahead of them, "Who are you, sir? And where does this path go?"

"My name is Vain Confidence. This path leads to the Celestial City," he replied.

"I told you so," Christian smiled, looking at Hopeful. They followed the man.

When night came, they could no longer see him ahead. Suddenly they heard a cry and a loud crash. Vain Confidence had fallen into a deep pit, put there by the owner of the meadow. Christian and Hopeful called out to him, but there was no answer.

Then it began to rain and thunder with terrible lightning. Christian was very sorry he had convinced Hopeful to take this easier path.

"Let's turn back," he said, trembling. "Perhaps we can find our way again."

Then they heard a voice saying, "Return to the narrow way." Christian and Hopeful tried to go back, but it was so dark and the water began to rise so high that they nearly drowned. Finally, they found a shelter and sat down under it. The weary pilgrims fell asleep.

Not far from where they slept lay Doubting Castle owned by a giant named Despair. The next morning he found Christian and Hopeful asleep on his property.

"You have no right to be here," the giant said in a loud, gruff voice. "Come along with me!"

Despair forced them to go with him, grabbing and

pushing them across the fields. He locked them in a very dark, dirty, and smelly dungeon. They were miserable, without anything to eat or drink from Wednesday to Saturday.

Giant Despair had a wife whose name was Diffidence. She didn't trust anyone or anything. She was cruel and told her husband to beat the prisoners. So, the next morning Despair used a huge club to beat Christian and Hopeful so hard they could not even move. They spent all that day and night lying there, weak, hungry, and moaning with pain.

The next morning, Giant Despair mocked them. "Why choose to keep living since you are in such awful pain?" he said coldly, telling them it would be better if they just killed themselves.

The pilgrims pleaded, "Please, let us go!" This made the giant so angry he rushed at them to beat them up again. But, before he got to them, he had a fit of weakness and could not use his hands at all. So, he left them there.

Christian said, "We are so miserable and in so much pain. Dying seems a better choice than living like this!"

"But the King says, 'You shall not murder,'" Hopeful said. "How much more then are we forbidden to do what Giant Despair says and kill ourselves?" For Despair was living up to his name, trying to discourage the pilgrims so they would lose hope and disobey their King.

"Let's be patient, and endure this for a while. We may be released. But let us not be murderers." Hopeful continued to encourage his friend. "Hold on a little while longer," he said. "Maybe our great God—remember he made the whole world—will cause Giant Despair to die, or Despair may forget to lock us in next time, or we may be able to slip away if he gets another fit of weakness." And with that, Hopeful convinced Christian to hold on to hope.

Giant Despair found them barely alive the next morning and he went into another terrible rage. The pilgrims were filled with fear once again.

Christian even fainted.

After Giant Despair left them, they talked again about suicide. Hopeful argued against it a second time, saying, "Remember what you've already gone through and survived. Apollyon couldn't destroy you. You made it safely through the Valley of the Shadow of Death. And you showed great courage at Vanity Fair. And I am a weaker man than you are, Christian. Let's be patient a little longer, as patient as we can be."

That night Diffidence told her husband to take the pilgrims to see the bones and skulls of those he had already killed. "Tell them that within a few days, you'll kill them, too," she said, with a mean look on her face.

When morning came, Despair showed the pilgrims the bones and skulls in the castle yard and told them he was going to kill them. Then he yelled, "Now go! Get back to your cell. Your end is coming!" With that, the giant punched and beat them all the way back to the prison.

They were very weak and faint. But then they began to pray, and they prayed all through the rest of the night. Christian suddenly spoke up. "How foolish I've been!" he cried. "We've stayed here all these days when we could have walked out freely!

"I just remembered! I have a little key in my coat, next to my heart. It is the key of Promise. I'm sure it will open any lock in Doubting Castle," he said. He tried it on the dungeon door. And with that, the bolt gave way and the door flew open!

Christian and Hopeful escaped quietly out to the iron gate. The key opened that lock also. But as they opened the gate, it creaked so loudly that it woke up Giant Despair. Just as he tried to run after them, Despair had another fit of weakness and fell to his knees, unable to move. The two friends hurried from the castle and ran across the field to the steps by the fence.

When they crossed back over to the narrow way, they found a large stone and placed it at the steps to warn pilgrims who would come after them. The message on the stone said, *This path in By-Path Meadow leads to Doubting Castle, which belongs to Giant Despair. He hates the King and tries to destroy pilgrims!* Many pilgrims who came after them read what they wrote and escaped that danger.

After this, Christian and Hopeful continued their journey on the narrow way. They sang about the King's deliverance and their adventures as they went.

# CHAPTER TEN

## *Shepherds and the Delectable Mountains*

he pilgrims kept walking and began to climb up some mountains. They were named the Delectable Mountains because they were beautiful, filled with all kinds of delicious, mouth-watering fruit trees, delightful gardens, vineyards, and fountains of water. They began to talk to some shepherds who were feeding their flocks there.

"Whose mountains are these?" Christian asked. "And whose sheep feed here?"

"These mountains belong to the King," replied one of the shepherds. "You can see the Celestial City in the distance. These sheep also belong to him. He laid down his life for them."

"Is the way to the Celestial City safe or dangerous?"

"It's safe for those who seek after the King. But some stumble in it," said one of the shepherds.

"Is there a place here where pilgrims may rest?" Christian wanted to know.

"Oh, yes. The King told us to take care of his people who come by here. Please stay here a while to get to know us better. We want you to find comfort here," said one of the shepherds.

The four shepherds were pastors named Knowledge, Experience, Watchful, and Sincere. They asked questions about Christian and Hopeful's journey and gave them a tasty meal. They prepared comfortable beds for them.

In the morning, the shepherds led them on a walk across the mountains to see more of their beauty. Along the way, they also took them to three places that were warnings to pilgrims. They came to the top of a steep hill called Error, which means wrong belief. The pilgrims looked down and saw the bodies of those who had died when they fell from the top.

The shepherds explained, "People sometimes leave the narrow way and wander up here alone to get a better view. They come too near the edge of this mountain called Error, fall off, and are killed."

Next, they went to the mountain of Caution. They saw people stumbling around like they were blind in the far distance. "What does this mean?" the pilgrims wanted to know.

"They are some of Giant Despair's victims at Doubting Castle. If he does not kill them, he puts out their eyes and leaves them to wander around blind until they die."

Christian and Hopeful looked at each other and began to cry. They knew they had come very close to the same thing happening to them.

Then the shepherds led them into a valley where there was a door in the side of a mountain. They opened the door and asked the pilgrims to look in. They heard a rumbling noise like a fire and someone screaming in pain. It was very dark and the smell of smoke and brimstone nearly choked them.

"This is a door to hell," the shepherds said, "for all those who hate the gospel, for hypocrites and pretenders like Esau who sold his birthright, and Judas who betrayed Jesus."

All these things made the pilgrims think hard. "Is it true that at one time each one of these people *wanted* to go on a pilgrimage?" Hopeful asked slowly.

"Yes," answered the shepherds.

The pilgrims looked at one another and said, "We had better look to the Strong One, Jesus himself, for strength."

"You will certainly need that strength for the rest of the journey," the shepherds agreed.

"Now let's show them the gates of the Celestial City and let them look through our binoculars," the shepherds said excitedly. They took Christian and Hopeful to the top of a high hill called Clear and let them look toward the Celestial City. In the distance, the pilgrims thought they saw something like a gate. The beauty of the place dazzled their eyes!

Next, one of the shepherds gave them a note with directions for the rest of the narrow way. Another warned them to be careful of the Flatterer. The third told them not to sleep on the Enchanted Ground, and the fourth said, "May God lead and protect you as you travel!"

Christian and Hopeful went down the mountains along the road toward the City. Soon, they came upon a lively young man named Ignorance. He came from the city of Conceit, walking on a crooked lane, to join the pilgrims on the narrow way. He said he was on his way to the Celestial City.

"You may not be able to get to the City," Christian told him. "The King's pilgrims must come in at the small gate and go to the Cross."

"Don't worry about me! I know God's will just as well as you do," Ignorance said. "I live a good life. I pay my debts. I pray and give offerings."

"But," said Christian, "you came in through that crooked path over there. I'm afraid that you will not get into the Celestial City."

"Stop making such a fuss!" said Ignorance. "You follow what you believe and I'll follow what I believe. We'll all make it in the end . . . I hope!"

Christian and Hopeful looked at each other. Ignorance was wise in his own eyes. Christian said, "A fool has more hope than he does." Then he added, "A fool lacks sense and shows everyone how unwise he is."

They decided to walk ahead of Ignorance and leave him to think about what they had said. Hopeful said, "I don't think we should tell him anything else right now. Let's give him time to think about what we've said." So they both went on ahead, and Ignorance followed behind them.

# CHAPTER ELEVEN

## *Little-Faith and the Flatterer*

s they walked, Christian told Hopeful a story. "Once a man called Little-Faith was on the narrow way and fell asleep. Three robbers named Faint-Heart, Mistrust, and Guilt came up and with threatening words, ordered him to get up. Afraid, Little-Faith didn't have the strength to fight or run away. The robbers grabbed his money and beat him with a large club. The robbers heard someone coming. Scared it might be Great-Grace, they ran away. Little-Faith finally continued on the narrow way."

Hopeful asked, "Did the robbers take all he had?"

Christian replied, "No, they didn't find his jewels. But they got his spending money. After that, he had to beg for food as he went, just to stay alive. I was told that he complained all the time about what had happened to him," Christian sighed.

"At least he was different from a man named No-Faith," Christian went on. "No-Faith was someone like Esau who sold his birthright to Jacob. No-Faith was willing to sell his soul to the Evil Prince. When he wanted something, he would do anything in the world to get it. People without faith are like that. They sell everything, including their own lives, so they can do sinful things.

"So there is a difference between No-Faith and Little-Faith," Christian continued. "No-Faith had no faith at all. On the other hand, Little-Faith had saving faith in the King and so even though his faith was small, he could not sell his soul or his jewels."

Hopeful asked, "But why didn't Little-Faith have more courage to fight against the robbers?"

Christian replied, "If you had been in the same situation, you might not have done well either. I've been in this sort of battle. It was terrible! I had my armor on, but I still had a hard time. No one knows how tough the fight is unless he has been in the battle himself!"

"Why did the robbers run away when Great-Grace was close by?" Hopeful wanted to know.

Christian replied, "Great-Grace is the King's champion, and he is able to win against robbers like these. There is a difference between the King's champions and Little-Faith. They are all pilgrims, but not all pilgrims are the King's champions. Some pilgrims are strong, and some are weak. Some have great faith, and some have only a little.

"But even Great-Grace and the King's champions like David, Peter, and Paul have scars and wounds from their battles against robbers and the Evil Prince. You may remember that Peter boasted he would never deny Jesus. But when Jesus was arrested, that's what Peter did.

*King David*

"Satan and his robbers are strong enemies," Christian warned. "Let's not think we can do better than others when we hear they have been defeated.

"Hopeful, we must remember two important things:

1. Go out with our armor strapped on. Above all, we must take the shield of faith!
2. We must remember that the King goes with us, and desire his presence more than anything else.

"As for me," Christian said thoughtfully, "only by God's goodness am I alive today. I can't boast that I won because of my strength.

"And I don't think we are out of danger yet," he went on, looking around. "I pray that God will deliver us from the next enemy we might meet."

As they continued the journey, Ignorance followed some distance behind. They came to a fork in the road. The two paths ahead appeared to be straight and narrow. Christian and Hopeful didn't know which one to take. A man in a very light robe appeared.

"Where are you going?" he asked.

"To the Celestial City," said Christian. "But we're not sure which is the right road."

"Follow me," said the man. "I'm going there, too."

So they followed him, and found him very agreeable as they talked together. He led them step after step, and in time they came to a bend in the road. It curved away from the Celestial City, and before they knew what was happening, the man led them right into a horrible net.

Just then the shiny robe fell off his back and there stood the enemy of the King. Christian and Hopeful lay there weeping, for they were trapped in the net through their own wrong choice.

"We were wrong to follow him," cried Christian. "Didn't the shepherds warn us about the Flatterer, someone who would tell us what we wanted to hear and agree with everything we said just to get us to do what he wanted?"

"Yes," Hopeful said sadly. "Besides, we forgot to read the directions the shepherds gave us."

A Shining One came toward them. They told him about the evil man and what happened. "It is the Flatterer," the Shining One explained. "He is the Wicked Prince. He transforms himself into an angel of light so he can tempt pilgrims to leave the narrow way."

The Shining One cut open the net and freed Christian

and Hopeful. Then he disciplined them for their foolishness, like a good father does to a disobedient son or daughter.

"I correct those I love," the Shining One said. "So be alert and repent." Then he sent them on the right path, instructing them to pay attention to the shepherds' map and directions. The pilgrims thanked him and went on their way singing.

They soon met another man named Atheist. Hopeful whispered to Christian, "Let's be careful because he might be a Flatterer, too!"

Atheist asked, "Where are you going?"

When they told him, Atheist laughed loudly. "You are ignorant to go on such a difficult journey," he said. "There is no King and no such place as the Celestial City."

"We have both heard and believe there is such a place. We believe the truth of God's Word and walk by faith in Jesus," the pilgrims said firmly.

Then Christian whispered to Hopeful, "Is what this man saying true?"

"No," warned Hopeful. "He is one of the Flatterers we were warned about. Remember what it cost us the last time we listened to someone like him? Besides, we saw the Celestial City when we were standing on the Delectable Mountains!"

So the pilgrims turned away from Atheist and continued on the narrow path.

# Chapter Twelve

## Hopeful's Testimony, Ignorance, and the Enchanted Ground

opeful started to get very sleepy. Christian, shaking his friend's arm, exclaimed, "Remember, the shepherds warned us about the Enchanted Ground. We must stay alert!"

"What would have happened to me if I'd been by myself?" Hopeful wondered. "I'm thankful you are here with me!"

Christian said, "To keep us from falling asleep, let's talk. Hopeful, what made you begin thinking about the things of God?"

Hopeful replied, "For a long time I was excited about all the worldly things in Vanity Fair. I enjoyed my sinful ways like swearing, lying, and cheating. Then you and Faithful said that these things ended in death and

God's judgment."

Christian asked, "Did you feel convicted or recognize that the things you were doing were wrong? Did you feel guilty about your sin?"

Hopeful replied, "No, at first I wouldn't even admit that what I was doing was sinful, and I didn't believe that I would be punished for it. I tried to forget that part. I didn't realize it was God who was working in me, showing me how sinful I was. You see, I enjoyed my sin and worldly friends too much and didn't want to give them up."

"What would bring your sins to your mind again?" Christian asked.

Hopeful replied, "Many things, such as
1. meeting a good person in the street,
2. hearing someone read from the Bible,
3. a headache or feeling sick,
4. knowing that some of my neighbors were sick,
5. going to a funeral,
6. thinking about dying,
7. hearing that someone had died suddenly, and
8. thinking that I would have to face God and his judgment for my sin.

"Finally, I decided I would try to fix my life. I

stopped the sinful things I was doing and didn't hang out with my sinful friends. I started praying, reading, crying about my sin, and speaking the truth instead of lying. And for a while I thought I was improving, but it wasn't working."

"Why not?" Christian asked.

"Some of the things you and Faithful said from the Bible kept coming into my mind. I began to think that if all my good deeds are only like filthy rags in God's sight, then no one, including me, can be saved by keeping the Ten Commandments," Hopeful explained. "I recognized that even my finest efforts and good deeds can't pay off the debt I owe God, and sin is mixed in with the best of the things I do."

"What did you do then?" Christian asked.

Hopeful replied, "I told Faithful about my struggles. He told me about Jesus, who had never sinned. Faithful said that I needed Jesus' righteousness, and that my good deeds could never save me. His words sounded strange at first. But once I started seeing my own weakness and sin, I knew he was right. I asked Faithful more about Jesus. He explained that Jesus had died on the cross to pay for my sin, and that Jesus would give me his righteousness if I believed in him."

"What happened next?" Christian asked.

"I made excuses," Hopeful said. "I thought that Jesus was not willing to save me since I had been so sinful. But Faithful told me that Jesus had invited me to come to him.

"Faithful gave me a book about Jesus to encourage me. He told me to ask God, with all my heart and soul, to show me Jesus, saying, 'God, I am a sinner. I need Jesus to save me. I can't do it on my own. Please have mercy on me, and give me faith to know and believe in Jesus Christ as my Savior. Please save me through your Son, Jesus.'"

"Did you do that?" Christian asked.

"Yes, I prayed over and over again," Hopeful said. "But nothing happened for a while, and I was tempted to stop praying. But, I kept praying until God the Father showed me Jesus. Of course, I didn't see him with my physical eyes, but with the eyes of my understanding. One day I was very sad because I saw how awful my sin was. But, suddenly, I understood that Jesus was speaking to my heart and saying, 'Believe on me, and you will be saved.'

"I told Jesus, 'I am a very great sinner.'

"And Jesus replied, 'My grace is enough for you.'

"Then I asked, 'Can I be truly accepted by you?'

"Jesus said, 'Whoever comes to me I will never drive away.' And Jesus is alive and always praying for me! I can't tell you how full of joy I was. I was so thankful to him for saving me and forgiving my sin. I loved everything about Jesus. I loved his wonderful name, his people, and all his beautiful ways. The Lord Jesus made me want to live a holy life, pleasing him, and bringing honor and glory to him."

After their conversation, they saw Ignorance still

walking behind them, and waited for him to catch up.

"Tell us about yourself, Ignorance. How are things between you and God now?" Christian asked.

"I hope I'm doing well," Ignorance answered, "for I always plan to do the right thing, and I have good thoughts, including ones of God and heaven."

"Well, the demons think about God and heaven. But just thinking about them is not enough," Christian pointed out.

"They are *always* on my mind," Ignorance declared. "I have left everything for them."

"I doubt that you really have," said Christian, shaking his head. "Leaving everything behind is very difficult to do."

"My *heart* certainly tells me I have," Ignorance said.

Christian quoted, "The wise man says, 'He who trusts in himself is a fool.'"

Ignorance replied, "But this passage talks about an evil heart, and mine is a good heart."

"How can you prove that?" Christian asked.

"My heart tells me that I should have hope about going to heaven," Ignorance said.

"But God's book says that the heart can tell us something that isn't true," Christian said. "What your heart tells you has to agree with God's Word for it to be true. God's Word says that no one is righteous, no one does good, and that every desire of our hearts is evil from childhood. When we believe this, our thoughts are good because they agree with what God says."

"I will never believe that my heart is bad," replied Ignorance.

"Then you can't call your thoughts good. We have right thoughts when we believe that God knows us better than we know ourselves. God's Word also judges our behavior. God says man's ways are crooked, not good," explained Christian.

"Well, I know that!" Ignorance said loudly. "I do know I must believe in Jesus to be saved."

"But why do you think you must believe in Jesus when you don't see your sin or your need for him?"

"But I do believe!" Ignorance insisted. "I believe that Christ died for sinners and that God will save and accept me because I obey the Ten Commandments and do good works."

"I'm so sorry, Ignorance," said Christian. "Your kind of faith is

1. an imaginary faith;
2. a false faith;
3. a faith that justifies yourself, and does not make Christ the Savior and Justifier of sinners; and
4. a faith that deceives and lies to you.

"Saving faith is trusting only in Christ's perfect obedience to God's Law and his death on the cross for us when we could not do anything to take care of our sin," explained Christian. "True faith accepts Christ's righteousness only, and does not count on our own good works. We can't earn our way to heaven."

"What!?" replied Ignorance angrily. "Believing that we are only supposed to trust in what Christ has done without our being involved would cause us to sin even more and live as we please!"

"What you are saying reveals how much you don't know about true, saving faith," said Christian. "When we have saving faith in Christ alone,

1. our hearts are humbled and won over to God and to Jesus, and
2. we love Jesus' name, his Word, his ways, and his people.

"So, no one who trusts in Christ's righteousness wants to sin more or live as he pleases."

Hopeful said to Ignorance, "No person can know Jesus as Savior unless God the Father reveals him."

Ignorance replied, "That is your faith, but it is not

mine. And I know mine is as good as yours."

"Oh, Ignorance, be careful and take this seriously!" exclaimed Christian. "No one can know Jesus Christ unless God the Father reveals him. God gives the gift of faith by his grace and mighty power alone. Wake up! Confess your own sin, and turn quickly to the Lord Jesus Christ. Only Christ can deliver you from eternal judgment and hell!" exclaimed Christian.

"You are going too fast for me," Ignorance grumbled. "Go on ahead. I will walk behind you."

Christian and Hopeful warned him some more. Then they continued on.

"I'm sorry for this man," Christian said sadly. "He is foolish to reject Jesus. He will be the loser in the end."

They recognized that many people, many families, and even entire towns were like Ignorance. Then the pilgrims went on to talk about fear and its purpose in the lives of people.

Hopeful pointed out, "Fear can have a good purpose in a person's life, especially when he begins his journey to the Celestial City."

Christian agreed, "Yes, if it is the right kind of fear. God's Word says, 'The fear of the Lord is the beginning of wisdom.'

"Three things help us identify true or right fear," Christian continued. "Right fear

1. starts in a person who realizes he is a sinner, confesses his sin, and sees his need for salvation;
2. makes a person turn to Christ to be saved; and
3. creates great awe and respect for God, his Word, and his ways.

"Right fear keeps a person's heart tender toward the Lord. It makes a pilgrim afraid to turn away from Jesus, to dishonor God, or grieve the Holy Spirit."

By this time, the pilgrims were not very far along the Enchanted Ground. As they walked, they continued their conversation.

"How do people try to run away from true or right fear?" Hopeful asked.

"They think their guilt is from the devil, when it is really from God," Christian replied. "They also

1. harden their hearts,
2. only believe in themselves, and
3. think they are fine already, so they push the fears away."

Hopeful nodded, "I was like this myself, before I knew what God said about my sin."

Then Christian asked, "Why do you think some people start out well, then they slide back into their old sinful ways?"

Hopeful answered, "There are at least four reasons people backslide:

1. Their minds have not been changed. They only want to go to heaven because they are afraid of going to hell.
2. They fear what people will think of them.
3. They think highly of themselves and believe religion is lowly and shameful.
4. They avoid thinking about the terrors of hell or their sin, and so harden their hearts, choosing ways that will harden them even more."

"Yes, you have said it well," Christian replied. "At the root of it all, they are unwilling to change their minds and their wills. They are like the thief who stands before the judge. He is sorry that he was caught, but not sorry that he broke the law and stole. When he gets out of jail, he will continue to be a thief. If his mind were changed, he would be different and stop stealing."

"How do people backslide?" Hopeful asked.

Christian answered carefully, "There are nine steps that people who backslide take.

1. They try to forget about God, death, and the judgment they will face;
2. then, they gradually stop praying, controlling their sinful desires, being watchful, being sorry about their sin, and other things;
3. they avoid friendly, enthusiastic Christians;
4. then, they stop hearing, reading, and discussing God's Word;

5. they criticize other Christians and say terrible things about them;
6. after that, they spend more and more time with worldly people who love to sin;
7. they give in secretly to worldly, bad habits;
8. then, they begin to do sinful things publicly in front of everyone;
9. finally, they show themselves for who they really are because their hearts are hardened.

"Unless God works a miracle of grace in their hearts," said Christian, "they will perish forever because they have lied to themselves about the consequences they will face."

Finally the two friends got across the Enchanted Ground. And soon they found themselves in the Land of Beulah, where the air was sweet and lovely!

# CHAPTER THIRTEEN

## *The Pilgrims Enter the Celestial City*

hristian and Hopeful liked the Land of Beulah very much. Beautiful birds were singing. Lovely flowers grew everywhere. The sun shone night and day. This bright country was far from the Valley of the Shadow of Death and the reach of Giant Despair. It was on the border of heaven.

Drawing near the City, they got a better view of it. It was an amazing place built of pearls and precious stones and paved with streets of gold! "Oh, I can hardly wait to get there!" Christian cried out.

Both pilgrims longed to go there so badly, they became a little sick. They were homesick for their real home in heaven and had to take a rest to get their strength back.

The two friends spent many happy days in the Land of Beulah. They ate delicious food and slept so sweetly.

When they awoke, they got ready to go up to the glorious City. As they walked on, they met two Shining Ones. "You have only two more difficult things to go through," they said, "and then you'll be in the City."

Between the pilgrims and the gate of heaven was a deep river, and there was no bridge to get across. Christian and Hopeful were crushed when they saw what lay ahead. The Shining Ones said, "You must go through the river, or you cannot get to the gate."

"Is there another way?" they asked, looking at the dark waters.

"Yes, but there have only been two pilgrims ever, Enoch and Elijah, allowed to go to heaven another way. You may remember that they were taken straight to heaven and did not die."

Then the two, especially Christian, began to despair. "Is it deeper or shallower in some places?" Christian asked fearfully.

"You will find it deeper or shallower depending on how much you trust the King," they answered.

So Christian and Hopeful started across the river. Right away, Christian began to sink. "The water is going over my head! I am sinking in deep waters. All the King's waves are going over me!" he cried.

"Don't be afraid," said Hopeful. "I can feel the bottom and it's good ground to walk on."

Christian said with distress, "I'm going to die in

these dark and horrible waters. I'll never make it to the Celestial City!" With that, a great darkness and horror fell upon Christian, and he could not see in front of him. He couldn't remember any of the wonderful things that had happened on his journey. His mind was filled with fear. The horror of his past sins, the things he did both before and after he became a Christian, rose up before him. And he thought he saw evil spirits coming to get him.

It was all Hopeful could do to keep his friend's head above water. Sometimes Christian would go under and then come up again, almost dead.

Hopeful kept comforting him. "Dear friend, we are close now, and men are standing by to welcome us."

"They are waiting for you, not me," Christian said. "From the day I met you, you have always been hopeful."

"Have you forgotten what the Bible says?" Hopeful asked Christian, holding him firmly. "These deep waters do not mean that God has left you. He sent them to test you to see if you will remember his wonderful goodness to you throughout your journey. The King wants you to depend on him in your suffering."

Christian began thinking hard about what Hopeful said. Hopeful reminded him of God's promise, "Be of good cheer; Jesus Christ makes you whole."

And with that, Christian was not as afraid anymore. He said with a loud voice, "*Now* I remember his promises. God's Word says that when I pass through the waters, he'll be with me. And when I pass through the rivers, they will not drown me!"

The enemy, the Wicked Prince, was quiet then and left them alone. For Satan had been the one tormenting Christian with all those awful thoughts. God restored their courage and they continued across the river.

Suddenly, the pilgrims found the river to be very shallow. They walked to the other side, and there they found the Shining Ones waiting to help them the rest of the way.

The Celestial City stood far above, higher than the clouds. But the pilgrims climbed up there quickly and easily because the Shining Ones held onto their arms, talking about how magnificent and marvelous the King and his heavenly home were.

"What will we do in the holy place?" the pilgrims wanted to know.

"When you get there," the Shining Ones said, "you shall receive white robes and crowns of gold. You will see your wonderful King at last, and walk and talk with him every day. There, you shall serve him all eternity, praising him and thanking him for who he is and all he did in saving you and bringing you safely to the Celestial City!"

The Shining Ones reminded the pilgrims that once in their new home, they would no longer be sad, sick, or troubled and there would be no more death, just as God's Word says. "God will give you joy and comfort, and you will be rewarded for all your hard work," they said. "You will see the good results of all your tears, prayers, and suffering for the King.

"And," the Shining Ones concluded, "you will enjoy family and friends who have gone on to heaven before you, and the ones who arrive there after you."

Now as Christian and Hopeful were drawing close to the gate, they saw Ignorance once more. He had crossed the river without difficulty. A man named Vain-Hope had given him a ride across in a boat. Once on the other side, Ignorance had climbed up to the gate alone because there was no one there to help him.

Ignorance knocked, and some men looked over the top of the gate. They asked him for his rolled document so they could take it to the King. But, of course, he did not have one and he had nothing to say.

Sadly, Ignorance had thought he could get into heaven without going to the Cross and trusting in Christ alone to save him. He was sure he had enough good works to earn his way in.

The King then instructed two Shining Ones to seize Ignorance, tie up his hands and feet, and take him away. They carried him to the door in the side of the hill, the door that led to hell. They shoved him in, and Ignorance was not seen or heard from again.

As Christian and Hopeful drew near the gate, a huge crowd came out to meet them. The two Shining Ones with Christian and Hopeful explained to the crowd, "When these men were in the world, they loved the Lord Jesus and left all for his precious name. Jesus sent us to bring them into the City. How happy they will be to see their wonderful Savior face to face."

Everyone gave a great shout of praise to the Lord. Others played their trumpets joyfully. It was a wonderful welcome indeed!

Christian and Hopeful arrived at the gate. "These pilgrims have come from the City of Destruction," the Shining Ones called out to Moses, Elijah, and others who were looking over the top of the gate. "They trust and love the King!"

Then Christian and Hopeful turned in their documents, which were brought to the King. When the King read them, he told his servants to open the gates and let the pilgrims enter.

The gates were opened and the bells of the City rang out with joy. Christian and Hopeful were given robes that made them shine like the sun. Crowns covered with sparkling jewels were put on their heads. Many more people were waiting to welcome the two men. "Come! Share in our King's happiness!" everyone cried.

So Christian and Hopeful were brought before the King, who was sitting on his throne waiting to receive them. Then they, along with all God's people and the angels in heaven, began singing, "To him who sits on the throne and to the Lamb be praise and honor and glory and power, for ever and ever!"

They shouted his praises, singing over and over again, "Holy, holy, holy is the Lord God Almighty."

After that, the gates were shut. Everyone in the whole City was glad that Christian and Hopeful had been brought safely from the City of Destruction all the way to the Celestial City. Their pilgrim journey was over. Now they were in the presence of their wonderful King forever!

# GLOSSARY

## ❂ CHAPTER ONE

**book:** God's Word, the Bible

**burden:** sin, with its weight and guilt

**Christian or pilgrim:** a man who repented of his sin and put his trust in Jesus alone to save him; God's people

**City of Destruction:** where all sinners live who have not put their trust in Jesus to forgive their sin

**Evangelist:** a loving, caring preacher of the gospel

**Obstinate:** stubborn, unwilling to change

**Pliable:** easily bent, easily influenced; only wants a gospel that makes him happy

**rags:** sinfulness, unrighteousness

**scroll:** God's Word

**Shining Light:** the Bible, which tells the truth about Christ

**Wicket Gate:** Christ and the salvation he offers

## ❂ CHAPTER TWO

**Civility:** someone who tells other people that they can get rid of their burden (sin) and earn their way to heaven by living a highly respected, good life

**Help:** a faithful believer who encourages those who are learning about their sin and the Savior; shares God's promises with them

**Legality:** believes and teaches that salvation can be earned by obeying the Ten Commandments and doing good works

**Morality:** trying to earn salvation by being good enough

**Mr. Worldly Wiseman:** loves money, comfort, and position, but rejects the salvation Christ offers; wants to take the easy way out of life

**narrow path or way:** the Christian life; God leads his people along the narrow way through this world to their home with him in heaven

**Slough** (*slew*) **of Despond:** the fear, carelessness, and unbelief that comes from the inside of a person; Christian becomes discouraged and almost despairs of getting out of this swamp because his sins are so great

**steppingstones:** God's promises to save and forgive a sinner through Christ

# ❋Chapter Three

**arrows:** lies of Satan that try to hurt and destroy Christians

**beautiful clothes:** Christ's perfect righteousness given to Christian when he puts his trust in Jesus at the Cross

**Celestial City:** heaven

**Cross:** where Jesus shed his blood to save us from our sins

**Evil Prince, Beelzebub:** Satan, the devil

**Goodwill:** our heavenly Father, who welcomes burdened sinners with grace and mercy

**Interpreter:** the Holy Spirit who is at work in a sinner's heart, opening his or her eyes to understand the Bible and Christ's payment for his sin; lives inside a believer, teaching and guiding him or her

**King:** Jesus Christ

**mark on Christian's forehead:** signifies a believer is set apart as a true child of God

**Place of Deliverance:** the Cross; the place where Christ delivers Christian from the burden of sin and guilt

**sealed document:** assurance of salvation, new life in Christ, and acceptance into the Celestial City; also Bible

**seven rooms of the Interpreter's House:** important lessons to help pilgrims on their journey
1. *picture of a man hanging on the wall:* a faithful pastor who leads others through hard times
2. *dusty room sprinkled clean with water:* Christ alone through the gospel can clean up a sinner's heart so that Jesus can enter and give him a new heart.
3. *two children named Passion and Patience:* Two attitudes— Passion is greedy and impatient; he can't wait. Patience is willing to wait on what God has for him.
4. *burning fire:* Satan tries, but fails, to put out the fire of faith; Christ pours out his grace (oil) on Christians to strengthen them for the journey in this life.
5. *beautiful palace:* a view of what heaven will be like; the Celestial City, the final home, by the grace of God, of faithful pilgrims after they have gone through many hardships
6. *Caged Man:* someone who hardened his heart against Christ and rejected him for so long that now he can't and won't believe
7. *trembling man:* a warning to be ready for God's final judgment

**Shining Ones:** angels sent from God; God's messengers

**wall called Salvation:** Christ's protection and assurance that the way forward for Christian is sure and certain

# ❋CHAPTER FOUR

**armor:** spiritual weapons God gives believers so they can fight against the devil and other enemies of Christ

**armory:** storage place for everything Christian needs to trust and serve God as well as face attacks from the enemy

**Charity, Discretion, Piety, Prudence:** mature believers who teach and encourage new believers in their journey
  *Charity,* love and kindness
  *Discretion,* wise and careful judgment
  *Piety,* faithfulness and godliness
  *Prudence,* good sense

**Graceless:** Christian's name before he believed in Jesus

**Hill of Difficulty:** hardship or struggles that Christians experience in their lives on their journey to heaven

**House Beautiful:** God's people, the church

**lions:** those who persecute Christians and test their faith

**Mistrust and Fearful:** false pilgrims; they are afraid and give up when faced with trouble

**paths of Danger and Destruction:** ways that God's Word warns against; not the Lord's way; in the end they completely destroy those who follow them

**study:** a place where Christian is shown the wonderful heroes of the faith from the Old Testament and other treasures found in God's Word

**Watchman of the house:** a church leader who warns, encourages, and guides believers

# ✸Chapter Five

**All-Prayer:** one of the main weapons to fight Satan and other enemies; God arms his people for battle against Satan through his Word, his presence, and prayer

**Apollyon:** Satan; also called the Destroyer, the devil, and dragon in the Bible

**arrows:** lies, deceitful accusations, and attacks hurled at pilgrims by Satan

**shield:** faith; part of God's armor that he provides for Christians to put on and use

**sword:** Word of God; offensive weapon that believers are to use; it is God's mighty power

**Tree of Life:** eternal life; God's life-giving, eternal blessings

**Valley of Humiliation:** a place of battle where Christians are taught to rely on God and his Word, not on themselves

**Valley of the Shadow of Death:** a place of fear, hopelessness, and darkness where pilgrims learn to walk in the strength of the Lord, depending on him alone

**Wicked Ones:** evil spirits

# ❋CHAPTER SIX

**Discontent:** never happy with anything; tries to get Christians to turn away from following and trusting Jesus

**Faithful:** a true believer whom God gives Christian to walk with him on the narrow path

**Mr. Conceited and Mr. Pride:** proud of their own talents and actions and do not fear the Lord

**Mr. Shame:** tries to make Christians embarrassed about following Jesus and doing what is right

**old man:** the old sinful nature

**Talkative:** false pilgrim; someone whose life doesn't match his words; he talks a lot about religion, but doesn't trust and obey Jesus

**woman:** any person who tries to trap Christians into sinning; worldly traps; does not mean that only women are sinful

# ✸ CHAPTER SEVEN

**Envy, Mr. Greedy, Mr. Old Man, Pick-thank, Superstition:** Satan's servants or helpers; in turn they represent jealousy, always wanting more than they need, the sinful nature, self-importance, and believing false ideas

**Judge Hate-Good:** chief servant of Satan; hates the truth and everything that is good

**Lord of the Fair:** Satan, the Wicked Prince

**Vanity Fair:** a place of worldly pleasures, where Satan tempts and persecutes God's people

# ✸ CHAPTER EIGHT

**Demas:** encourages people to go after the things of this world; a warning against loving money rather than trusting and loving God

**Fairspeech:** a town of pretenders, liars, and deceivers

**Hopeful:** a true believer whom God brings into Christian's life to encourage him in his Christian walk

**Lot's wife:** someone who loves this world most of all; a disobedient and greedy heart

**Lucre:** money or wealth that is gotten by dishonest means

**Mr. By-Ends:** a false pilgrim of Fairspeech who uses religion to gain riches, knowledge, high position, and an easy life

**Mr. Gripeman, Mr. Hold-onto-the-World, Mr. Money-Love, Mr. Save-all:** false pilgrims and friends of By-Ends who cheat, tell lies, and pretend to be religious

**Plain Called Ease:** a place or time of rest, peace, and contentment that God gives believers along the way to heaven

# CHAPTER NINE

**By-Path Meadow:** appears to be an easy way out from the struggles and responsibilities of the Christian life, but in fact leads believers to doubt God and get discouraged

**Diffidence:** distrust

**Doubting Castle:** a place of uncertainty, doubts, and fears; not sure who or what to believe

**Giant Despair:** feeling depressed, discouraged, sad, and hopeless; can happen when Christians doubt God and don't trust and obey him

**key of Promise:** the promises of God; Jesus delivers his people from doubt and despair when they seek him in the Word and in prayer

**Vain Confidence:** false hope

# CHAPTER TEN

**Delectable Mountains:** a place of rest, comfort, and teaching; the local church

**door in the side of a mountain:** the way to hell for hypocrites, pretenders, and all those who hate the gospel and do not put their faith in Jesus

**high hill called Clear:** gives a view of the Celestial City as seen from the Delectable Mountains to encourage pilgrims who are on their way to heaven

**hill called Error:** a warning not to believe or follow false teachings or things that God warns against in his Word that lead to destruction

**mountain of Caution:** a warning to be careful not to stray from the Christian path that leads to life, to learn from the mistakes of others and be thankful for God's grace and mercy

shepherds named **Knowledge, Experience, Watchful, and Sincere:** a picture of the qualities found in a godly pastor and in other Christian leaders, teachers, and parents whom God gives us

## ❉ CHAPTER ELEVEN

**Atheist:** a false pilgrim who doesn't believe that God exists; an enemy of Christ

**Flatterer:** Satan, the Wicked Prince; pretends to agree with everything Christians say; Satan's evil forces who try to deceive Christians, tempting them to leave the narrow way

**Great-Grace:** one of the King's champions; by his grace God has given some Christians greater faith

**King's champions:** strong Christians with great faith who also have scars and wounds from their battles against Satan and his evil forces

**Little-Faith:** a Christian who is not alert and watchful and so loses his strength and courage, but who does have saving faith in King Jesus

**No-Faith:** someone who does not trust in Jesus as Savior and who is willing to sell everything he has to Satan, even his own soul, to keep on sinning

**pilgrims in a net:** the consequences God's people suffer when they sin; a trap of error and pride

**robbers named Faint-Heart, Mistrust, and Guilt:** inward struggles faced by Christians who must look to the King for faith and deliverance

## ❉ CHAPTER TWELVE

**Enchanted Ground:** a place designed to mislead the hearts and minds of Christians so that they stop paying attention to the things of God

**Ignorance:** a false pilgrim from the city of Conceit, a place of pride and self-importance; a person who talks about Jesus, but has never trusted in Christ alone to save him; one who trusts in his own obedience to save him

## ❖CHAPTER THIRTEEN

**hell:** the final place of torment or separation from God for all those who refuse to repent and believe in Jesus Christ as their Savior and Lord

**Land of Beulah:** a time of peace and hope often experienced by Christians toward the end of their journey

**river:** death and trials that some Christians go through when they are dying; death is the last great enemy Christians experience before entering heaven

**sealed document:** assurance of salvation, new life in Christ, and acceptance into the Celestial City; also Bible

**Vain-Hope:** false hope, useless

**Wicked Prince:** Satan

# ❊ GLOSSARY INDEX ❊

# ANNA TRIMIEW

**Anna Trimiew** is a curriculum and children's writer who approached this adaptation of Bunyan's story with great care. It was of utmost importance to her that the biblical truths shine through clearly to children as they become immersed in this grand story of imagination and adventure.

Trimiew, who was born in Kingston, Jamaica, is a former elementary school teacher. She came to the United States to earn her B.A. from Florida State University and has a master's degree in Theological Studies from Gordon-Conwell Theological Seminary. Her work includes *Bringing the New Testament to Life* (Cook), *Bible Lessons in LessonMaker* (NavPress), and *The Get-Well Activity Book for Kids* (Harold Shaw Publishers). She has been a curriculum writer for Great Commission Publications for the past 16 years, writing multiple departments of the *Show Me Jesus* children's material, *So What?* youth Bible studies, and *Kids' Quest Catechism Club.* She has also written the accompanying *Kids' Quest Pilgrim's Progress* curriculum for grades two through five.

# JOHN L. MUSSELMAN

**John L. Musselman** is an author, teacher, and former pastor who has been teaching *The Pilgrim's Progress* to disciple men for more than 20 years. He is a scholar of Bunyan and his work, and has written a modernized version and study guide of *The Pilgrim's Progress* for adults. As the theological editor, Musselman provided crucial guidance, insights, and dedication.

Musselman is the president of the Jackson Institute, a leadership development organization in Atlanta whose mission is to contribute to the cultural, intellectual, and spiritual formation of individuals who are on a passionate quest to be welcomed, received, and acknowledged by God.

Born in Griffin, Georgia, Musselman graduated from the University of Alabama with a B.S. in Mathematics in 1972. He received his M.Div. from Reformed Theological Seminary in Jackson, Mississippi and the D.Min. from Fuller Theological Seminary in Pasadena, California. Prior to his founding the Institute in 1991, he served on the staffs of Coral Ridge Presbyterian Church in Fort Lauderdale, Florida, Evangelism Explosion International, and Perimeter Church in Atlanta. Musselman is the author of *Youth Evangelism Explosion, Classic Discipleship,* and *The Holy Spirit and His Gifts.* He has also edited two other classic Christian works: *The Training of the Twelve* by A. B. Bruce and *Man's Chief End* by Thomas Watson.

# DREW ROSE

**Drew Rose** is an accomplished illustrator whose passion for this project was apparent from the start. "I asked the Lord to send me a special project," Rose has explained. "My heart and soul went into this book for 11 months. I put aside everything because this was a labor of love and I knew this was something I wanted to contribute to God. Whatever is done for Christ will last."

Born in Châteauroux, France, Rose knew from childhood that he was an artist at heart. He would often immerse himself in libraries for hours, pouring over the work of the great artists from the golden age of children's book illustration. Determined to illustrate professionally one day, he attended Virginia Commonwealth University and obtained a B.S. degree in Communication Art and Design.

For the first 15 years of his career, Rose produced art for the U.S. Postal Service and many of America's leading corporations, including Coca-Cola, McDonald's, Apple, Frito-Lay, Purina, and a host of others. He has since dedicated his talents to book and children's illustrations. He works in an ink undercoat surmounted by a very tight wax-colored pencil rendering, which allows light to pass through the transparent topcoat and bounce back to the eye, producing brilliant life and color. His preferred subjects are the boundless world of a child's imagination: pure, untouched, and full of wonder. He has received many honors, including the Weatherspoon Gallery award and an ADDY award.

# PILGRIM'S PROGRESS
## CURRICULUM

*Download FREE samples*
**www.childrenspilgrimsprogress.org**

Teacher's Manual

Music and Dramatic Reading CDs

*On the Go* student papers

*On the Go Plus* for upper elementary

**GREAT COMMISSION**
**PUBLICATIONS**

3640 Windsor Park Drive
Suwanee, GA 30024-3897
800-695-3387 • www.gcp.org